T3-BUV-786

California Weight Loss Program

BY H.S. JUDD
written with James M. Terrill, Ph.D.,
Psychologist Evelyn Langenwalter,
Registered Dietitian

A KANGAROO BOOK
PUBLISHED BY POCKET BOOKS NEW YORK

Distributed in Canada by PaperJacks Ltd., a Licensee
of the trademarks of Simon & Schuster, a division of
Gulf+Western Corporation.

POCKET BOOKS, a Simon & Schuster division of
GULF & WESTERN CORPORATION
1230 Avenue of the Americas, New York, N.Y. 10020
In Canada distributed by PaperJacks Ltd.,
330 Steelcase Road, Markham, Ontario.

Published by arrangement with Simon and Schuster,
A Division of Gulf & Western Corporation
Library of Congress Catalog Card Number: 76-1425

ISBN: 0-671-81481-8

First Pocket Books printing April, 1979

10 9 8 7 6 5 4 3 2 1

Trademarks registered in the United States and other countries.

Printed in Canada

Congratulations!

You are about to begin a nine-day Weight Loss Program that can show you how to control food to end your weight problem permanently

This program works because it combines the latest psychological techniques with tested, food control principles. You lose weight while you learn the solid basics of eating a balanced nutritional combination of foods.

This program is no fad diet. You don't give up the foods you are now eating. You go on eating the same foods your family eats while you learn to *control* the amounts of the foods you eat. You are mastering a total food control program you can use the rest of your life to increase your chances for continued good health. You are not forcing yourself onto some dull, restrictive, temporary diet of only one or two foods to try to lose weight. On this program, you need never be more than a day away from a portion of your favorite high calorie food, whatever it is. That's right! Ice cream, baked potatoes, avocados, butter, cakes, pies, pastries, candy — whatever your craving, you can earn the rewards of having it while you are losing weight.

How To Use This Program Successfully

You will get best results if you follow exactly the instructions for using this program. The program has been carefully designed so that you can use it in the privacy of your own home.

Don't try to 'jump ahead' in the program or do more than one lesson per day. You will only hurt your own chances for success if you do so. Each lesson is designed to teach you one or more important principles of permanent food control.

You should read *only one lesson a day* and you should really spend the rest of the day thinking about what you have learned. Your objective should be to *master* these weight loss techniques completely so that you don't have to think consciously about them any more. Just like riding a bike, you will use them *automatically* every time you eat foods or drink liquids.

However, you don't have to wait nine days to start benefitting from this program. You can start right now. In the back of this book you will find a pocket-size weight loss program outline. You can begin immediately to follow the three rules and fifteen steps to *permanent* weight control. You will find thirty-four WEIGHT CONTROL REINFORCEMENT CARDS. Cut them out and begin using them today to start mastering your control over the food you eat.

You can also begin to reward yourself for losing weight by earning Weight Loss Credits. You do this in the following way. Use your WEIGHT LOSS CHART to record your weight each evening before you go to bed. Each day that you lose one or more pounds or do not gain one or more pounds, pay yourself with a Weight Loss Credit. When you have earned two Weight Loss Credits, you may reward yourself with a portion of one of the foods listed on the SET-BACK FOOD LIST.

Start your program now by reading the introduction and Lesson One. Follow the instructions in each lesson but *do not do more than one lesson each day.*

GOOD LUCK. There is no reason why, after learning these techniques, you cannot slim down to the weight you want to be and stay there permanently. And don't worry if after starting out well you then fall down or fail along the way. One of the real benefits of this program is that it *plans for you to fail along the way*, but this time, you will be *failing successfully*.

This program will give you all the information you need to succeed in mastering food control. The time it takes to reach your weight loss goal is up to you.

Contents

		Page
Introduction		1
Lesson 1.	Admitting the Problem	7
Lesson 2.	Deciding to Change	11
Lesson 3.	Completing Your Personality Profile	15
Lesson 4.	Personal Problem Solving	19
Lesson 5.	Writing Your Contract	29
Lesson 6.	Starting Your Program	43
Lesson 7.	Reaching Your Weight Loss Goal	53
Lesson 8.	Why the Weight Loss Program Works for You	59
Lesson 9.	Controlled Fasting and Other Helpful Techniques	75
Questions and Answers		83
Personality Profile		89
Daily Reinforcement Cards		101
The 5-Point California Weight Loss Program		125
Set-Back Foods List		127
Weight Loss Charts		129

Introduction

Your first step toward positive personal growth is self-acceptance

---

Are You Enjoying Yourself?

You may ask what that question has to with losing weight. The answer is that it has *everything to do with losing weight* or with any other program you select to change yourself and your life style.

Do you feel good about yourself? Do you love yourself? Do you accept yourself? Do you have a high self-image? Are you O.K.? This question can be asked in many ways, but basically it boils down to the kind of person you *believe yourself to be*. Before you can master the techniques of the CALIFORNIA WEIGHT LOSS PROGRAM, you have to take a good long look at yourself. This program works because it is based on psychological and physical principles which work *because you accept yourself.*

Using Food To Solve Your Problems

Most of us who are overweight are using food to solve personal problems. Our problem may be insecurity, emotional stress, loneliness, fear of losing a job, lack of personal goals, a dread of growing older, or one of many other fears or anxieties. Whatever the problem, many of us rush to the refrigerator to calm ourselves with beautiful fattening food. Actually, that isn't a bad way to reduce physical tension. Eating is a pleasure, and the food tastes good. The problem is that it doesn't reduce our waistline. We pay for our overeating with excess weight which can lead to sickness, heart trouble and other physical problems, not to mention the daily physical strain extra weight puts on our body.

Therefore, your weight problem may be a *symptom* rather than the *problem* itself. And unless you can dig in and deal with whatever it is which is driving you to the refrigerator, even if you *do* lose weight, you won't be solving your real problem.

There are two general approaches to personal problem solving. One approach is to reach back into your past with a practicing psychotherapist and seek out those events which may have caused your present problems. Another way to change your life style is to substitute new 'mental images' for your old habits, to decide where you want to be and work toward the future rather than try to work backward to the cause of your present problem.

This approach assumes that each of us is 'O.K.' and has just as much right to enjoy happiness and success in life as anyone else. This approach recommends accepting yourself totally as you are with all the things you like and don't like about yourself. The things you don't like you change through a planned program which is aimed at establishing new habit patterns.

By using this approach, we all start out equally, whatever it is we may have done in our past. We 'let go' of all the negative things which have been programmed into us over the years. We accept the fact that the past is gone forever, but that we can decide what happens to us tomorrow by paying attention to what we are doing right now.

The Importance of Attitude

Many people continually fail in their repeated attempts to lose weight because they approach the problem in an excessively self-denying, repressive way. When you do this, you spark off a 'civil war' between your over-strict conscience (or inner parent) and that part of you that drives you to overeat. Whenever this happens, the part of you that drives you to overeat often rebels and overthrows the overly strict conscience. You then usually overrespond by rejecting yourself and vowing to try harder next time, thus setting up the conditions for still another failure.

The CALIFORNIA WEIGHT LOSS PRO-GRAM approaches this problem from the point of view that successful, permanent weight loss can occur only when you can accept and under-stand what is behind your urge to overeat. Once this has been accomplished, there will be less chance of an inner 'civil war' developing and weight loss should go much more smoothly.

In practice, this will mean that you will need

to spend considerable time getting acquainted with the *overeater* in yourself before you begin to master your total control of the food you eat. Hence, much of the first half of this program is concerned with helping you to develop a compassionate understanding of the tensions and needs that underlie your pattern of overeating.

Once you have done this, you will need to attempt to provide harmless non-fattening ways to take care of the frustrations, needs and insecurities that you have previously tried to relieve through overeating.

Even though you may not be able to provide non-fattening outlets for all these tensions, at least you should be able to lessen the degree to which the overeater in yourself will need to rebel and fight back against your attempts to change. In other words, show the overeater in yourself that you understand and will try to take care of these needs, and the overeater will be more apt to cooperate with your weight loss plan.

Summary

This program was designed to give you techniques you can use to solve your weight loss problem permanently. You won't find any fad diets or quick weight loss diets here. What you *will* find is a program you can use to eliminate your weight problem.

What you will be doing is building a sound program which includes ways to handle temporary failures, food binges and other setbacks along your way to final success in 'controlling' food rather than having food 'control' you. You will learn a nutritional food program to follow to lose weight. NOTICE, WE DO NOT RECOMMEND A *DIET*! We show you techniques to use to lose weight quickly through food control.

This CALIFORNIA WEIGHT LOSS PRO—GRAM is a way to lose weight which does not require a strict, repressed program of self-denial. Rather, it suggests ways you can learn to change your attitude toward yourself and your attitude toward food. When you change yourself and your attitude toward food, you may no longer want to be fat. Once you have reached this decision, you will lose weight because you want to, not because it is something you *must force* yourself to do.

On the other hand, this program may convince you that you enjoy being fat. If you are one of those people, and after taking a look at the real risks of being overweight, you still decide you'd rather be fat, THEN YOU HAVE EVERY RIGHT IN THE WORLD TO ENJOY YOURSELF EXACTLY THE WAY YOU ARE. The choice is yours.

Admitting the problem

If you don't identify the problem correctly, you won't solve it

---

Forget everything else you've read about losing weight and dieting. Clear your mind. For the moment, we're not even going to think about food or diets or calories. We're going to concentrate on YOU.

You are a unique individual. Not in 10,000,000 years will another person come along with your exact characteristics. Therefore, unless we start out from *your point of view*, we can't hope to come up with a weight loss program that will work. What works for me may not work for you. What works for you may not work for your neighbor.

Each of us has our own unique problems which put extra pounds on us. The extra pounds make us fat. The problem which causes our fat may be simple and it may be complex. Whatever it is, we can solve it if we really want to.

Remember, being overweight is one of the easiest problems to correct once we decide *we want to lose weight.* You may not believe that now, especially if you've tried for years to lose weight and failed, but by the end of this week you'll agree that losing weight is a minor problem compared to some of the problems you could have.

Ask Yourself, 'Why Am I Fat?'

Before you can work up your personal weight loss program, you have to *know* why you are fat. Once you know that, you are well on your way to success. Remember, being fat is being seven pounds or two hundred pounds overweight.

Now take a pen or pencil and fill in Section One of your PERSONALITY PROFILE. *Do not read further in this lesson until you have completed Section One of your PERSONALITY PROFILE.* After you have done this, return to this lesson.

You should now have completed Section One of your PERSONALITY PROFILE. Study carefully what you have written. If you have been honest with yourself, you should now have a pretty good idea what causes you to overeat. If you have been honest with yourself, it is a good sign you really want to lose weight.

If you haven't been honest with yourself or can't think of any reasons why you are fat, you may not really want to lose weight. If this is so, if you really don't have any motivation to change, then chances are you won't change. The best thing you can do in this case is to forget about losing weight and enjoy yourself the way you are now. That's right! Some people simply don't want to lose weight. If you are one of them, why not enjoy it? But remember, you don't *have* to be fat. You can change yourself and your life and enjoy it more if you want to.

Don't go on to Lesson Two until tomorrow. Spend the rest of today thinking about why you are overweight. Imagine yourself the way you would like to look. Then ask yourself if you are willing to pay the price to change. Are you sure, absolutely sure, you really want to change or would you rather stay the way you are right now? The answer you come up with to this question will determine whether you will lose weight or not.

DO NOT GO ON TO LESSON TWO UNTIL TOMORROW

Deciding to change

If you don't really want to change yourself, you won't

O.K., you now have a pretty good idea why you are fat. At least you have several reasons why you think you are fat. In other words, you think you know why you are where you are now. This is your starting place. Where you want to be is your goal. If where you want to be is different from where you are now, you can't get there unless you *change*.

Following Your Personal "Being Fat" Script

Imagine yourself a famous theatrical star playing in a long run on Broadway in New York. Each evening you come into the theater, put on your make-up, and go out on the stage to play your role. Each evening you follow the same script and the play ends exactly the same way. Each new audience sits in suspense, wondering what will happen, knowing that the same thing will happen that happened the night before, but enjoying the experience.

Well, you are living your life exactly the same way, you are starring in your own 'being fat' script. Think about it. You get up in the morning determined to change yourself, determined to lose weight. Some days you succeed, others you don't. The point is that you are continually frustrated by your attempts to change. You stay the same. You stay the same fat person you tell yourself you really don't want to be.

How can you change then?

Before you can hope to change yourself, you first have to change your 'being fat' script to a 'being slim' script. Ask yourself — Who controls my mind? Am I controlled by life or do I control my own life?

CONTROLLED BY LIFE

Let's go back again to the Broadway star. The Broadway star goes out each evening and performs because the performance results in personal rewards — fame, money, artistic achievement, entertainment, career, security and so on. With a lousy script, audiences wouldn't come and the play would close down. The star would search around for another role. In other words, you are being rewarded for playing in your own 'being fat' script. If you really want to change, you have to close down your 'being fat' play, rehearse your new 'being slim' role and open your new 'being slim' production.

You are still being paid for being fat.

Now turn to Section Two of your PERSON-ALITY PROFILE. Answer the questions in this section. Take no more than thirty minutes to do so. Fill in the rewards you feel you are getting for being fat.

Don't continue reading this lesson until you have completed Section Two of your PERSON-ALITY PROFILE.

Review

- You have now come up with reasons why you think you are fat.
- You have now listed reasons why you think you are being rewarded for being fat.

Now you are going to have to list new rewards you will get by losing weight.

This is a key point. It may be the reason you have failed to lose weight so far. *A negative goal is never a real goal.* This means: "I want to stop smoking" and "I want to lose weight" are not real goals. In fact, they are self-defeating.

A real goal is an objective you want to reach

because you desire a real reward. There is no reward in self-denial. In other words, you may have been failing so far in your attempts to lose weight simply because you haven't stated your goal properly.

By replacing a negative goal like "I want to stop smoking" with a positive goal like "I want to save money and feel healthier and younger and I will earn these rewards by not smoking," you aim yourself toward a desirable goal instead of away from an immediate reward.

In order to successfully change, you must want the new reward more than you want the reward you are now getting from the habit you want to break.

You have already written down the rewards you get now from being fat. Review the first two sections of your PERSONALITY PROFILE. It is important for you to understand why you are overweight and what rewards you are getting from overeating.

Spend the rest of today trying to think about the rewards you want to earn by losing weight.

DO NOT GO ON TO LESSON THREE
UNTIL TOMORROW

Completing your Personality Profile

Changing your life is like going on a trip. You have to know where you want to go, where you are starting from, and whether or not you have the resources to get there.

You are now about to complete the most important single section of your PERSONALITY PROFILE. In Section Three, you are going to list the rewards you want to earn by losing weight. As you complete this section, don't worry about how you are going to get these rewards. Don't worry about the cost or anything else, just list what you *really* want out of life.

Now turn to Section Three of your PERSONALITY PROFILE and complete it. Come back to this lesson after you have finished Section Three.

You Must Now Make An Important Decision

You have written down the rewards you now get from being fat. You have listed the rewards you will get from losing weight. You must now decide which rewards you really want.

This is the hardest, most difficult decision you will have to make in your weight loss program. But think about it. This is the basic decision you have to make about your weight all your life. Do you want to be fat? Or do you want to be slim? Think about your decision carefully. Before you go on with this lesson, make your decision. If you decide to stay the way you are, this program will have given you an understanding of why you prefer being fat. At least you should be able to stop fooling yourself and enjoy yourself the way you are. But if you want the pleasures of being slim, the rest of the program will show you how to reach that goal and stay there. The choice is yours. *Do not go on until you have decided whether you really want to lose weight or stay the way you are now.*

If you have decided to lose weight, the rest of this program will show you how to do so *permanently*. If you have decided that the rewards are greater by losing weight, congratulations! You are going to look better, feel younger and enjoy life more than you would if you chose to stay fat.

Be absolutely honest with yourself because the more honest you are, the better able you will be to successfully complete your own personal weight loss program. If you are wondering why it takes all this time to 'plan' your way to losing weight, remember all those times you 'jumped' into a 'fad' diet only to be back at your old weight a week or a month later.

Planning Is Your Key to Success

The work you are doing now is vital to your success. Unlike diets that start you off immediately counting calories or studying why your body physically puts on or takes off weight, this program starts and ends with *you*. The mechanical process of losing weight is simple. It is the psychological change you must achieve to break the habit of overeating that takes the planning.

As you fill out the rest of your PERSONALITY PROFILE, remember that it is your foundation to your successful weight loss program. If you have filled it out honestly, it will be a totally unique profile. That's why your personal weight loss program has the greatest assurance of working. You will be following a program designed specifically for you.

Now complete Section Four of your PERSONALITY PROFILE and return to this lesson after you have done so.

Do not continue reading until after you have completed your PERSONALITY PROFILE.

You now have in hand a profile that outlines why you have a weight problem. It tells you what rewards you are now getting by staying overweight. It tells you what rewards you will earn by losing weight. It also shows you your 'pressure periods' (times when you 'stuff' yourself more than usual). It shows you the 'danger foods' or 'dynamite foods' or 'empty calorie foods' you like which put on weight fast. It shows you your weight loss goal. Don't go on to the next lesson until tomorrow. Review your PERSONALITY PROFILE. Remember to stand back and watch yourself while you are eating. Think about how you eat, what you eat and why you eat when you do.

DO NOT GO ON TO LESSON FOUR
UNTIL TOMORROW

17

Personal problem solving

Clear the major stress situations out of your life

O.K., you have taken time to complete your PERSONALITY PROFILE. What do you do now? If you have filled out your PERSONALITY PROFILE honestly, it should give you a pretty good idea what your major personal problems are. It is important now to stop and take a good long look at your personal situation. Generally a person will have a tough time trying to concentrate energy on solving more than one major problem at a time. Your job is to determine the relative importance of your losing weight to any other personal problem you may have.

As we said, more often than not, overweight comes from using food to solve problems. The key to your success in losing weight will be your ability to substitute an alternative problem-solving method for eating.

In the first lesson we discussed the importance of self-acceptance and your progress toward the person you want to be. It is now important for you to decide whether this is the right time for you to start this weight loss program. Timing, as sports stars well know, is vital to success in improving personal performance. You want to be sure that you time your weight loss program to begin under the best possible conditions.

How Can You Determine If Your Timing Is Right?

Your first decision is whether you are facing any other *major personal problem* or not. For example, have you just lost your job? Are you in the middle of a divorce? Has someone near to you just died or is someone very sick? Are you having major problems with someone at your office or in your family? If so, if you have any major personal conflict which you can identify, it is probably best for you to deal with that problem and solve or *at least resolve* it before you start out on your weight loss program.

Another example of timing would be not to start your weight loss program a week before Thanksgiving or Christmas or a week before you leave on your vacation or move to another part of the country. A third example would be not to start your weight loss program a few weeks before some major event (your daughter's wedding, a job change, etc.). The point is that you should be reasonably sure that you have cleared your life of any major stress situations before you start out to lose weight.

Read through your PERSONALITY PROFILE once more and then come back and read the following six options we suggest you consider before you continue your weight loss program.

Now review the following six options. See if you fit into one or more of these situations. They are, of course, generalized, but apply to most of the problem-solving areas in which people find themselves.

Option 1 — You are O.K.

After reviewing your PERSONALITY PROFILE, you believe that you have no major problem to deal with. You want to lose weight and you feel you are ready to start the weight loss program. You have looked at where you are right now and where you want to be, and other than wanting to lose weight and slim down, you are generally pleased with your present situation. You accept yourself.

Recommendation: Continue the CALIFORNIA WEIGHT LOSS PROGRAM. Follow the instructions carefully and slim down to the weight level for which you are aiming.

Option 2 — You have identified one or more major problems in your personal life right now.

You *must* pin down exactly what the problem is. Generally, major personal problems fall into one of the following areas:

a. *Low Self Esteem*
  - Lack of confidence
  - Changing moods
  - Expectation of failure
  - Belief that others are 'better' than you are
  - Feeling of isolation, inferiority

b. Insecurity
- Free floating anxiety
- Feeling something terrible is going to happen
- Fear of world situation, doom
- General state of nervous worry

c. Relationships With Other People
- Frustrating relationships with parents, friends, spouse, children
- Difficult marriage relationship
- Poor social relationships
- Unhappy relationships with fellow workers

d. Survival
- Threats to your life, imagined or real
- Threats to your life style
- Threats to your family

e. Financial
- Fear of loss of income
- Fear of loss of job
- Fear of not being able to survive at your present level of income
- Fear of not having skills to earn sufficient income

f. Health
- Fear of sickness
- Fear of death
- Fear of mental breakdown
- Fear of nervous breakdown

g. Self Expression
- Fear of growing old
- Fear life is passing you by
- Fear you are not being 'true to yourself'
- Fear you are wasting your life
- Fear you are not living the life you really want to live

If after reviewing your PERSONALITY PRO-
FILE, you really feel you have a major problem
in one of the areas listed above or in any other
area not mentioned, then it is possible that
unless you resolve this problem your weight loss
program may not achieve the results you desire.

Recommendation: Get a blank piece of paper,
or more paper if you feel you have more than
one major problem, and in a single sentence,
state specifically what your problem is. Then
try to solve or resolve it, listing all possible
solutions.

For example, suppose you list your major
problem as a financial one. You decide your
major problem is:

I Am Afraid of Losing My Job
1. List all the reasons why you are afraid of
   losing your job, for example:
   - I am getting too old to do the work
   - My job is being replaced by a computer
   - My company is going out of business
   - My boss dislikes me
2. List all the things you think you can do
   about your problem, for example:
   - I can look around for a new job
   - I can retire
   - I can switch to a different job
   - I can change my boss's opinion of me
3. Decide whether you can solve this problem
   by yourself. Ask yourself, "How can I
   solve this problem?"

This is an objective, scientific approach to
problem-solving. This system can help you
enormously in solving or resolving personal
problems.

Here are the steps again:

Step 1: What is my problem? Write out the problem in a single sentence.

Step 2: Why is this a problem? List all the reasons you can think of.

Step 3: How can I solve this problem? List all the solutions you can think of.

Step 4: Could I solve this problem better with outside professional help? Be very careful to consider this option. Don't consider cost.

Step 5: Make your decision. Select one of the solutions you have come up with and try it. If it doesn't work, try another.

Now if you are resolving this problem and it is no longer a major problem in your mind, go ahead and start your weight loss program. But if you are not able to resolve it and you still want to start your weight loss program, then follow the recommendation in the next option.

Option 3 — See if you can substitute another way of dealing with this problem besides eating food.

Now that you know *what your problem is* and you recognize that it very well may be the cause of your overeating, it is possible you can deal with it while you are losing weight.

Recommendation: Ask yourself how you can relieve the stress this problem is causing you without turning to food. Is there nothing you can *substitute* for food? Is there another way you can personally 'handle' the problem without overeating? Experiment for a few days. Try to substitute alternate reactions next time you enter a 'stress situation.' See if you can avoid the kitchen or the restaurant and substitute walking, a movie, a massage, a cup of coffee or whatever you can think of for the food you usually eat.

If you become convinced you can substitute another problem-solving method for overeating, then go ahead and continue your weight loss program.

Option 4 — You know the problem and you don't believe you can solve it yourself.

Recommendation: Go find the logical person to help you solve the problem. If it's a legal problem, see an attorney. If it's a medical problem, see a doctor. If it's a mental or an emotional problem, see a psychotherapist. Identify the problem area and then seek *professional* help. Don't avoid seeking professional help because you are afraid it will cost too much. The mere fact that you start the process of *solving your problem objectively* is a vital breakthrough and in almost all cases you will be able to find a way to benefit from professional help whatever your personal income.

Don't feel ashamed to seek professional help. All of us at one time or another in our lives find ourselves in personal situations requiring professional help. Remember, your objective should be to solve your personal problem as quickly and efficiently as possible. Use every means to do so. By bringing in a professional, you will benefit from years of experience, but better yet, from the objectivity which comes from dealing with similar problems throughout a career.

Option 5 – You either don't want to solve your problem or you don't want to face your problem.

There are many of us who find ourselves in less than perfect 'life situations.' In other words we realize that a relationship we have or a job we hold is not entirely to our liking; nor is it so intolerable that we want to walk away from it.

It is often this kind of a problem (one with no real 'yes or no' answer) which wears us down and leads to the emotional stress which puts on excess weight. By learning to live with our problem and deciding we would rather not solve it or eliminate it because the personal cost might be too high, we often find that life becomes less interesting and more difficult for us. In this kind of a situation, one of the most interesting, non-threatening things we can do to 'escape' the reality of our problem is to *eat food*.

Recommendation: You are going to have to decide what you want to do with your life. You can continue to go along the way you have. You can use any of the methods suggested in the first four options to deal with your problem and resolve it. You are really the only one who can make the decision for yourself. It's up to you. Try to analyze what it is you *really* want from your life and then try to decide what to do to get it.

But if you decide to continue to go along the way you have been going, at least you can now do so knowing that you have made a *conscious* decision to do so. This should enable you to accept yourself for what you are and better enjoy the life style you have decided to choose.

Option 6 — Your problem is 'unknown.' You feel you have a problem but you can't pin down exactly what it is.

This is a state sometimes called 'free-floating anxiety.' It can result from a number of minor stresses building up into a major undefined 'threat.' It can be caused by any number of things including an undiagnosed physical problem, a repressed trauma somewhere in your past, or a generally run down condition.

Recommendation: If your 'anxiety' is acute (if you're *really* suffering), get professional help. Otherwise, go ahead and continue your weight loss program. Losing weight and getting into a nutritional food control program may be just what it takes to get you back on the right track again.

Review:

Don't get bogged down in the problem-solving process or use these problems as an excuse not to lose weight if you really want to lose weight. Basically your problem will be one of five kinds of problems to solve:

1. You won't be able to identify your problem.
2. You will decide you can solve your problem by yourself.
3. You will decide you can solve your problem with outside help.
4. You will decide your problem can't be solved.
5. You will decide you don't want to solve your problem.

It is important to keep your major objective in front of you. Your major objective is to decide whether you want to lose weight or not. So don't get sidetracked or make the process more difficult than it is. Simply apply the techniques suggested here to identify your problems and resolve them. Then decide whether you really want to continue your weight loss program at this time.

Summary:

Before you continue your weight loss program, it is most important that you clear your life of any major stress situations. We have suggested six optional situations you may find yourself in and ways to resolve problems you may have. The more time you take now to analyze your present situation through study of your PERSONALITY PROFILE and application of the techniques suggested here, the better chance you will have that your weight loss program will work for you when you start out on it.

As we said before, the choice is up to you.

DO NOT GO ON TO LESSON FIVE
UNTIL TOMORROW

Writing your contract

Write your contract in the present, assume that you have the results now

---

You are now ready to write your personal WEIGHT LOSS CONTRACT. Without taking the time to complete your PERSONALITY PROFILE, you couldn't have written your contract. You now have probably spent more time in just four days studying your weight problem objectively than you have in years. This is a scientific approach to problem-solving. One of the things it does is separate *you* from your *problem*.

Your plan, your PERSONALITY PROFILE, are objective techniques to achieve measured results. The other aids you will have, your WEIGHT LOSS CHART, SET-BACK FOODS LIST, 5-POINT WEIGHT LOSS PROGRAM, DAILY REINFORCEMENT CARDS and WEIGHT LOSS GOAL CARDS, all assist you in solving your weight loss problem *objectively*.

One of the benefits of this program (as you may have guessed by now) is that you can use exactly the same process to solve other problems you may have. The more you practice these problem-solving techniques, the better you become at using them.

Your Contract In Writing:

Now let's take a look at your personal WEIGHT LOSS CONTRACT. When you complete and sign this form, you will have accomplished 75% of the hard work it takes to lose weight (and this hasn't been that hard, has it?).

You may be wondering, "Why do I have to fill out a form like this?" It is a good question. Remember, in order to succeed with your program *you must separate yourself from your problem. You must solve your problem objectively.*

The *mechanics* of losing weight this time are going to be easier for you because when you run into a 'failure point' or a 'difficult craving,' you are going to have your WEIGHT LOSS CONTRACT and GOAL CARDS to fall back on — written expression of what you really want which you can rely on when your emotions are driving you in the opposite direction.

Let's stop for a moment to mention one problem you are going to face. I know you are going to face it because you share this problem with every other person who has ever changed by breaking a habit. In order to break your eating habit, you are going to have to change your fat self. You are going to have to change that fat self that has been 'comfortable' inside you at your expense.

Now that fat self is going to fight back. That fat self is going to drive you to failure if it can. That fat self will tempt you and frighten you. Some of the symptoms you may get will include headaches, stomach aches, dizzy spells, fatigue, constipation, fear of getting sick because of your diet, shooting pains, nausea, feeling weak, anxiety and others.

If you are *really worried about any of these symptoms*, make an appointment to see your *doctor*. Check yourself out. Don't worry about being a bother to your doctor and don't worry about what it will cost. Your doctor knows that you can do nothing better for your present health than lose weight until you are operating at your proper weight. Losing excess fat is one of the best preventative maintenance programs there are for keeping in good health.

This weight loss program is designed to give you ammunition to fight back when your fat self is fighting you. That's why you have written down your PERSONALITY PROFILE, your GOAL CARDS, your WEIGHT LOSS CHART. When you need help, you've got it. Now take time to fill out your personal WEIGHT LOSS CONTRACT. Use your PERSONALITY PROFILE for the information you need. When you have completed it, sign it and date it.

The following is a sample of a contract filled out. Remember, state your rewards in a positive way. You are contracting to lose weight. You are contracting to gain the rewards that come from losing weight.

WEIGHT LOSS CONTRACT

NAME I. M. THIN   AGE 42

I am contracting with myself for the following rewards:

I FEEL BETTER, LOOK BETTER, HAVE A BETTER MENTAL ATTITUDE,
I LIKE MYSELF MORE AND HAVE IMPROVED MY SELF CONFIDENCE.
MY LIFE IS MORE INTERESTING AND EXCITING. PEOPLE
SHOW ME MORE RESPECT. I SLEEP BETTER AND WAKE UP
WITH ENTHUSIASM. I ENJOY EATING AND DO NOT STUFF
MYSELF TO RELIEVE TENSIONS.   ←

In order to earn these rewards I am paying the following price:

I have lost ___45___ pounds. I have stuck to my
weight loss program and persisted in spite of temporary failure. I have followed through until I have
reached my weight loss objective of _121_ pounds.
Along the way, I have paid myself with special rewards as follows:

AT 151 POUNDS I WENT TO THE MOST EXPENSIVE
RESTAURANT AND ATE ALL THE FOODS I LOVE.

AT 136 POUNDS I BOUGHT $300 OF NEW CLOTHES.

AT 121 POUNDS I SPENT A WEEK IN HAWAII.
      ↗   ↖

I will read this contract each morning when I get
up and each evening before I go to sleep.

SIGNED I. M. Thin   DATE 2/30/16

AS IF YOU ALREADY HAVE THEM

AS IF THEY HAD ALREADY HAPPENED.

3 SPECIAL REWARD LEVELS SET 15 lbs. APART

How To Figure Out What Your Permanent Weight Should Be

There are many systems for determining your weight level. The following guideline can be used to figure out where you should be at your best weight level. It works like this. You figure your permanent weight loss level by measuring your height. When you have established your weight loss level, your weight loss range can be either up to nine pounds less or nine pounds more than your weight loss level.

This gives you a range of up to eighteen pounds you can use to set the level *best for you.* You can slim down to the minimum level or stay up at a higher level if you prefer.

For Women

Measure your height in your stocking feet. Credit yourself with one hundred pounds for your first five feet. Add five pounds for each inch over five feet. This will give you your permanent weight loss level. Your actual weight can be either nine pounds less or nine pounds more than your weight loss level.

For example, suppose you are 5'5" tall. Your permanent weight loss level should be:

a. First 5 feet: 100 pounds
b. 5 inches times 5 pounds: 25 pounds
c. PERMANENT WEIGHT
   LOSS LEVEL: 125 pounds
d. WEIGHT LOSS RANGE:
   from a low of 116 pounds to a
   high of 134 pounds.

For Men

Measure your height in your stocking feet. Credit yourself with one hundred ten pounds for your first five feet. Add five pounds for each inch above five feet. This will give you your permanent weight loss level. Your actual weight can be either nine pounds less or nine pounds more than your weight loss level.

For example suppose you are six feet tall. Your permanent weight loss level should be:

a. First 5 feet: 110 pounds
b. 12 inches times 5 pounds: 60 pounds
c. PERMANENT WEIGHT
   LOSS LEVEL: 170 pounds
d. WEIGHT LOSS RANGE:
   from a low of 161 pounds to a
   high of 179 pounds.

When you have determined your permanent weight loss level, write down the amount of weight you want to lose to reach this level. You are now going to set your *special reward levels*.

In order to set your special reward levels divide the amount of weight you want to lose by three. For example, if you want to lose thirty pounds, set your special reward levels at twenty pounds overweight, ten pounds overweight and at your final weight goal.

Don't make your special reward levels more than twenty pounds apart or less than five pounds apart. For example, if you are eighty pounds overweight, set four special reward levels. If you are only ten pounds overweight, set only two special reward levels.

The important point is to set special reward levels at which time you pay yourself with a special reward for reaching an objective. It is *important* that you make these rewards attractive; something you really want to do, love to do. This even includes going out to dinner and eating all those fattening foods you've been giving up on your weight loss program.

If you can't afford 'money rewards' use your imagination. Pay yourself in other ways. Get someone in the family, a friend, an employer to pay you for reaching a special reward level. (For example, if you are poor, single, and without family or friends, talk to your employer. Tell him or her you are going to lose the fat you carry around with you and it will be good for him/her and for you. Get your employer to award you a 'special day off' when you reach each weight loss level. Your chances are excellent your employer will do so.)

Now look over the sample WEIGHT LOSS CONTRACT and then fill out and sign your own personal WEIGHT LOSS CONTRACT. (An extra form is included for a work copy.)

AFTER YOU HAVE COMPLETED YOUR WEIGHT LOSS CONTRACT COME BACK TO THIS LESSON.

WEIGHT LOSS CONTRACT

NAME _____ AGE _____

I am contracting with myself for the following rewards:

_____
_____
_____
_____
_____
_____
_____

In order to earn these rewards I am paying the following price: _____

I have lost _____ pounds. I have stuck to my weight loss program and persisted in spite of temporary failure. I have followed through until I have reached my weight loss objective of _____ pounds. Along the way, I have paid myself with special rewards as follows:

_____
_____
_____
_____
_____
_____

I will read this contract each morning when I get up and each evening before I go to sleep.

SIGNED _____ DATE _____

WEIGHT LOSS CONTRACT

NAME _____ AGE _____

I am contracting with myself for the following rewards:

_____
_____
_____
_____
_____
_____
_____

In order to earn these rewards I am paying the following price: _____

I have lost _____ pounds. I have stuck to my weight loss program and persisted in spite of temporary failure. I have followed through until I have reached my weight loss objective of _____ pounds. Along the way, I have paid myself with special rewards as follows:

_____
_____
_____
_____
_____
_____

I will read this contract each morning when I get up and each evening before I go to sleep.

SIGNED_____ DATE _____

You now have a document that will help keep you on target while you head toward your weight loss objective. Before going on a long trip, an intelligent driver makes sure he or she has an accurate map to follow. Before going into space, the astronauts worked out and carried with them written operation orders to get them safely there and back. Before any successful complex mission is accomplished, a written, workable plan must be completed. Did you have this plan the last time you tried to lose weight?

Well, you have it now. And you can use it successfully to reach your weight loss objective.

Study your contract. Read it tonight before you go to bed and tomorrow when you get up. Read it every day, at least twice a day and more often if possible. This represents your decision to lose weight permanently and it can be a powerful help to you when you drift into times where you have urges to go on 'food binges' or 'stuff yourself with fattening foods.'

DO NOT GO ON TO LESSON SIX
UNTIL TOMORROW

Starting your program

See yourself the way you want to be and you will get there

You may be thinking right now, "I am really ready to start this program. I have my contract signed and for the first time, I really believe I can reach my goal. Let's get started. Let's get going!"

Well the truth is that you started your weight loss program the moment you decided to buy the CALIFORNIA WEIGHT LOSS PROGRAM. You have been *planning* to lose weight and *searching* for a successful way to do it.

O.K., now you have the desire, the plan and the method. You've already started your program. From now on, it's going to be easier and easier, as long as you persist in your program.

It sounds simple, too simple, doesn't it? But you can do it. With a sound plan, you can gradually eliminate the anguish, frustration and failure which usually result from starting a program to change a habit without preparing yourself thoroughly for the job.

How do I know this can work for you? I know because human nature directs each and every person toward what he or she *wants* to do. Think about it. If you *want* to lose weight and you *want* the rewards you have set for yourself, you will lose weight as long as you continue to follow this program.

Filling Out Your GOAL CARDS

Now fill out your three GOAL CARDS. Write the goal exactly the same way on each card. Write your final objective. For example:

```
┌──────────────────────────────────────────┐
│              GOAL CARD                     │
│  I WEIGH 121 POUNDS & I FEEL GREAT!        │
│  I ENJOY LIFE MORE! MY FAMILY AND FRIENDS  │
│  HAVE MORE RESPECT FOR ME.                 │
│  I LOOK YOUNGER AND AM MUCH MORE           │
│  ATTRACTIVE THAN WHEN I WAS FAT.           │
│  I AM IN EXCELLENT HEALTH.                 │
└──────────────────────────────────────────┘
```

It is important to write your goal in the present as if you already have it.

Now keep one of your GOAL CARDS with you at all times, one by your bed, one in your purse or wallet, and one in the kitchen by the refrigerator. In odd moments, read and reread your GOAL CARDS. Read them as often as possible.

This will reinforce your psychological attitude toward your new self and away from your fat self. The more you read your GOAL CARDS, the easier it will be for you to change yourself.

Now fill out your WEIGHT LOSS CHART. Enter your weight each evening just before you go to bed. If you don't have a scale, use a tape measure and measure your waist. But be sure to enter your weight in pounds or inches each evening.

Each time you read your GOAL CARD, shut your eyes and 'imagine' exactly how you look and feel at your new weight. See yourself having fun, enjoying yourself. Imagine yourself as your new self.

The Technique of Visualization

This weight loss program is based on a positive, new philosophy of self direction toward *visualized* goals.

As children, teen-agers and college students, most of us have experienced the pleasant, secure and generally fulfilling life styles which result from aiming at specific goals. Remember how it felt to know that 'next year you will be a Senior'? Your life seemed to have *purpose*, *direction* and *meaning*. There were automatic 'rewards' for moving upward from first to eighth grade. There were 'traditions' — cheer leaders, football games, the Senior Prom. All of these things combined to provide an environment into which you fit and you could identify your role. You were the student.

It also established the teacher who *cared* about you. Whether you liked the teacher or not, at least you knew somebody *cared*.

For many of us, the day we graduate from our final school, we feel a real loss. No longer is the system looking out for us, telling us what to do. We're on our own. Some get married and start the process all over again through their children. But then when their children finally grow up and leave, they experience a sudden loss of security. They begin to question 'what is it all about?' and 'why are we here?' and 'where do I go from here?'

Fortunately, there is a wonderful, painless way we can create 'meaning' and 'direction' for ourselves. It is through *visualization*.

If You Can See It, You Can Be It

Motivational research has learned a great deal from the study of athletes. For one thing it has been demonstrated time and again that the performance of a star Olympic athlete often results from nothing more than concentration on a single desire. In other words, the champion did not start out with such exceptional talent that it automatically assured success. What was much more important in the champion's career was the dedication, the weeks, months and years of practice spent to get to the Olympics.

You can apply the same techniques to your own life. You can decide where you want to go and then *imagine* your way there.

It is important that you apply the visualization technique to your weight loss program. Select several 'mental images' of the rewards you expect from your weight loss. See yourself at your slim weight. See yourself enjoying activities which your excess weight has hampered. Visualize the reward you have selected to pay yourself when you reach your final weight loss goal.

At least once a day, either in the morning or evening, shut your eyes and take time to *visualize* the rewards you will get from losing weight.

Don't just spend a minute doing this. Actually daydream the experience. Move around in the experience. Feel it. Taste it. Make it a reality in your mind's eye.

Now select the reward you want the most. Practice seeing it so that you can shut your eyes and see it instantly. For example, suppose you have decided to spend a week in Hawaii when you have reached your weight loss goal. Practice until you can shut your eyes and instantly see yourself on a beautiful beach, feel the warm breeze, hear the ocean, see the blue sky and white clouds, hear the Hawaiian music, feel the joy of plunging into an ocean of warm salt-water.

You can use this image over and over again to keep yourself from slipping backward. Once you have selected your key reward every time you are tempted to do anything that will set back your program, shut your eyes and imagine your reward being shattered. It only takes a second.

The next time you start to sneak food not on your program, shut your eyes and imagine your reward being shattered. See it falling apart. As you keep doing this, you will find your desire to reach your reward will far overpower your occasional compulsion to stuff yourself with food. *Your key to success will be your visualization toward your major weight loss reward.* Once you have mastered this technique (and it is easy for you to do so) you will have a powerful resource to use to speed up your weight loss program and reach your final goal.

Additional Techniques

In addition to the techniques of visualization, there are a number of tested, helpful ways you can improve your effectiveness in reaching your ultimate weight loss goal.

All of these techniques are described here for you. All of these techniques have been included in your DAILY REINFORCEMENT set of cards. By selecting a different technique each day you can concentrate on mastering 'self control.' These techniques will be valuable to you not only for losing weight but in other areas of your daily living.

Remember, each of these techniques requires practice, patience and repetition. You are learning a new skill and don't expect dramatic and perfect results the first few times you use the technique.

1. Plan to Fail: Unless you are really exceptional, you will fail along the way to your weight loss goal. There will be days when your whole program goes to hell and you are really down in the dumps. You will be discouraged. You'll want to quit the whole thing. You'll probably stuff yourself with fattening foods to prove to yourself you are a failure.

Well, don't give in to self-pity and discouragement. Accept failure. Forget yesterday's failure and go ahead and succeed today. Think of champion boxers who have lost fights only to get up, train and come back to win again. Take an attitude of tolerance toward yourself and remember that everyone fails from time to time. Don't let one day's failure ruin weeks and months of success.

2. Take Time To Relax: At least once a day, try to get away in a quiet room and relax by yourself for fifteen minutes or more. Lie down and breathe deeply. Inhale and count to ten. Exhale and imagine all your tensions leaving your body. Repeat the process counting to nine, then eight, and finally down to one.

Make your period of relaxation a formal ritual. Try to do it at the same time each day. Use this time to review your day, practice your future success in avoiding fattening foods, and to get rid of personal tension.

3. Rehearse Your New Success Habits: Once you are completely relaxed, visualize situations in which you succeed in not eating fattening foods. See yourself substituting new success habit patterns for eating. Rehearse each situation in detail, seeing yourself walking past the bakery store or saying "no" when passing the french bread, or whatever your particular temptation is.

When you fail, rehearse the failure situation substituting a new way you avoid eating in that situation. Rehearse your way to a new life style which controls food.

4. Break Your Habit Pattern: Practice doing something else whenever you get a sudden urge to eat fattening food. Even if you cannot resist eating the food, at least do something else before you eat the food. If it's nothing more than walking around the block or taking a shower or simply counting to fifty before you stuff yourself, do it. By consciously breaking your *automatic habit pattern* you will be slowly building strength to eventually resist the compulsion to eat.

5. Reward Yourself Every Day: Don't put off all your rewards for the future. Pay yourself daily simply because you are determined to lose weight and get back to your normal healthy weight level.

Even on days when you fail, reward yourself. Use your imagination to pay yourself the rewards. They can be little things, taking time to relax, taking a walk, leaving the dishes in the sink overnight, going to a movie, anything which gives you a little boost and makes each day more interesting and enjoyable.

You Are Now On Your Way To Success

You now have an excellent personal plan, an understanding of the problem you are solving, and an excellent 'rewards' system set up for reaching your goal.

Congratulations: You now have a practical program to work with. Forget the temporary failures if and when they do come. Keep your eye on the new rewards of not being fat anymore.

In the next lessons you will be introduced to a nutritional *food control program* that not only helps you to lose weight but enables you to maintain your new weight loss level permanently.

DO NOT GO ON TO LESSON SEVEN UNTIL TOMORROW

Reaching your weight loss goal

You are not perfect

How are you doing? Are you reading your WEIGHT LOSS CONTRACT twice each day? Are you carrying your GOAL CARDS around with you? Are you recording your weight each evening before you go to bed? If you are doing these things, you are already losing weight whether it shows up on the scale or not.

Stop and think about it. Remember, your plan is your passport to success. You use it to reinforce your determination to change and to measure your progress. You follow it to reach the real rewards you have set for yourself.

How To Reach Your Weight Loss Objective

O.K., you are following your plan and you really want those rewards more than you want the rewards you are now getting from being fat.

Let's get into the mechanical process of losing weight. Let's look at what you have to do to lose weight. These are four possible situations; simple isn't it?

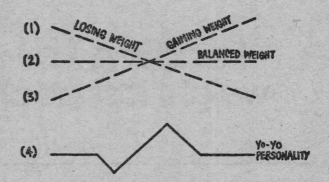

All you have to do is put yourself in situation one and you'll lose weight.

Up to now you've probably been convinced this 'dieting' business is complicated, requiring all kinds of mathematical calculations, counting calories, carbohydrates, etc. Well, forget all that. This program will give you an easy way to lose weight without counting anything. You need to follow only three simple rules, plus fifteen Do's, Don'ts and Do Without's. The question then is, "How can I get myself into situation one?"

If you stopped eating today and didn't eat anything for weeks or months, eventually you'd waste away to nothing. The mechanics are that simple. Stop eating and you will lose weight. What causes the problem then? The problem is caused by the fact that most of us simply can't, like some guru, retire to a mountain top and fast. We need energy; we need nutrition on a daily basis, so we eat.

And we usually eat the wrong combination of foods which keeps the weight on.

Losing weight is a chemical process. Your weight stays on or comes off because chemically the food you eat creates more energy than your body can use up and therefore stores it as excess fat. This happens because you are eating too much food. You can change that chemical combination by learning new eating habits.

The CALIFORNIA WEIGHT LOSS PROGRAM can work for you. Start out on it. Experiment. By following the program, you can lose all the weight you want to lose while assuring that your nutritional needs are being met.

A Secret Sign That Can Help You Like Nothing Else

Before we go into the food control program, here is a secret you can use to lose weight fast. Imagine two people waiting at an airport to take a jet to California. One is going out to California to start a new job with a top salary in San Francisco. The other is handcuffed to a policeman who is escorting him to a fifteen-year prison sentence. The same thing is happening to each person. They are both getting on a jet and going to California. But what a difference in how each is looking forward to the experience.

You should welcome the next hunger cravings you get because these hunger cravings tell you that you are losing weight. Up until now, you have probably dreaded those hunger cravings. They have probably driven you off diets and made you miserable when you failed. Forget all that. Now when you get a hunger craving, welcome it, because it means you are succeeding.

Besides, now you know how to deal with it. When you get it, drink a glass of water, read your GOAL CARD, concentrate on the rewards you are getting as you are losing weight.

O.K., what happens if you still go on an eating binge and fail? A good question. The answer? If you give in to an eating binge, enjoy every minute of it! But binge only for one meal or one hour, then get it out of your mind, pick up and start being careful again.

Remember, you are not perfect. Unless you are really exceptional, you are bound to fail along the way to reaching your final goal. *But this time you are going to be failing successfully*!

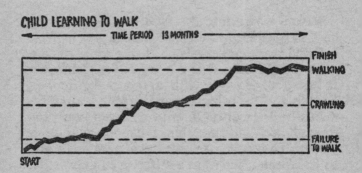

CHILD LEARNING TO WALK
TIME PERIOD 13 MONTHS

FINISH
WALKING

CRAWLING

FAILURE
TO WALK

START

Before you started this program, you probably didn't have a plan to follow. Giving in to an eating binge totally destroyed your self-confidence and made you a fool in the eyes of those who knew you were on a diet and caught you stuffing yourself in front of the refrigerator.

But this time, this temporary failure is only a sign that your plan *is working*.

One failure among days of continued success is not important. This time you are losing weight because twenty-four hours a day your plan is working for you. I guarantee that if you stick to your program and forget the temporary failures, you will succeed in losing the weight you want to lose.

Remember, it is through failure that champions achieve record breaking performances.

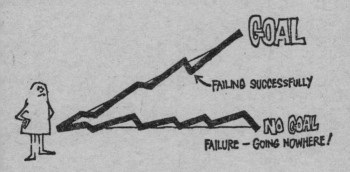

With a plan, your failures are temporary setbacks on your way to success.

As you select and follow the program outlined for you, remember that your objective is to establish a pattern of programmed eating. You are going to control your eating, your eating is not going to control you.

Be inventive. Enjoy your weight loss program and enjoy yourself the rest of your life as the slim attractive person you can be.

DO NOT GO ON TO LESSON EIGHT
UNTIL TOMORROW

Why the weight loss program works for you

You can lose weight and maintain your necessary nutrition level at the same time

---

Before we describe the program you can use to take off weight, let's stress the fact again that you *should consult with your doctor before starting out on any weight loss program.* Make an appointment and discuss your program with your doctor. It just makes good sense. You wouldn't (or shouldn't) make a big financial decision without checking with your accountant. If you had a legal problem, you would certainly contact your attorney.

The important thing to remember is that you should have sound medical advice before getting into your weight loss program if you're really serious about losing weight.

Your Food Control Planning

We recommend that you start out on a nutritional program of 'food control'. The first requirement of any good weight loss program is that it be nutritionally adequate. This program is not a fad diet. It is a method to approach food that will result in your mastering food control. You may find that when you apply the program you lose weight quickly. You will find that you begin to feel better as the pounds melt away. However, your quick weight loss will be the result of your control over food and not the result of a temporary fad diet.

This 5-Point Weight Loss Program plus your psychological techniques to change your eating habits are all you need to reach your weight loss objective. Moreover, by following this program you will be on a nutritional eating program which you will want to follow after you have reached your desired weight level.

After you have completed your PERSONALITY PROFILE, your WEIGHT LOSS CONTRACT, your GOAL CARDS and filled in your WEIGHT LOSS CHART, you are ready to begin your food control planning.

The success of this program rests on the fact that it is not a program of self-denial. As you lose weight, you will be able to eat in limited quantities those high calorie foods you love and which have caused your weight problem.

Why You Are Overweight

Though we won't go into great detail here, we will discuss the general process which leads to being overweight.

In order to function properly, your body needs three essential daily things: air, water and food. Life equals energy. Food is your body's energy source. Food supplies your body with three vital things:

1. The necessary energy to keep your body warm and to enable it to carry out its daily functions.

2. The basic structural materials for growth and body repair.

3. The carbohydrates, fats, protein, minerals and vitamins required to maintain the chemical balance in your body.

Your key to continued healthy living is a balanced diet. In order to make sure you are getting all the carbohydrates, fats, protein, minerals and vitamins you need, you must balance your daily diet with foods from the four Major Food Groups.

Being fat results from eating more calories than your body needs. The excess calories are stored as fat. Your success in getting rid of excess fat will result from your success in changing your food program to eliminate the intake of excess calories. Fortunately, we can accomplish this without having to go to extreme restrictive, calorie counting, repressive measures.

Once you get the hang of it, you can even enjoy eating your favorite high calorie food, ice cream, cheesecake, whatever it is you like.

Why Fad Diets Don't Work

Most people start out well on fad diets only to fall down after a few weeks. The reason — fad diets are not adequate nutritionally and they are generally boring, dull and unfulfilling. As soon as you jump into a fad diet, you are taking a real risk with your health. For unless your daily food program includes a *balanced* combination of food, you may be missing a protein, vitamin or mineral vital to your continued good health. In other words, you are not being properly nourished.

The Risks Of Being Fat

At the same time, being overweight does bring some real risks with it. Diabetes, arteriosclerosis, cirrhosis of the liver, cardiovascular renal diseases and increased risks during pregnancy and surgery are just some of the physical problems which can be made worse by being overweight — not to mention your own physical appearance, increased insurance costs, lower salary potential, low self-image, poor sleeping, lack of general enthusiasm for life and all the other annoyances which can result from being fat.

Nutritional Guidelines

The problem many of us have when we decide to lose weight is that we have never learned even the most basic rules of nutrition. Studies conducted by the U.S. Government, the U.S. Department of Agriculture and others indicate that millions of American families fail to eat the minimum daily allowances of carbohydrates, fats, proteins, vitamins and minerals recommended by the National Research Council. In other words, millions of American children, parents and older men and women simply don't know how to eat properly.

There is no mystery about nutrition. But many people try to make it complicated in their desire to keep on eating the non-nutritional foods they have been trained to enjoy while avoiding the foods they should eat to maintain good health.

Nutrition comes from eating foods from four primary food groups. These food groups are:

1. Meats, fish, eggs, beans and nuts
2. Dairy products
3. Fruits & vegetables
4. Breads & cereals

By selecting daily foods from each of these food groups, you assure that you get the nutritional benefits of the following kinds:

- Carbohydrates
- Fats
- Proteins
- Vitamins
- Minerals

You can be assured you are getting the nutrition you need if you balance your daily meals with foods from each of these four Food Groups. If you are pregnant or suffer any abnormal physical problem, you should see your doctor. You may need additional special foods to provide extra nutrition for a special condition.

Calories are simply a way of measuring heat or energy. When you overeat, as we have said, your body stores the excess heat or energy as fat. The principal sources of calories are carbohydrates, proteins and fats. Therefore, in order to lose weight, you must cut down on your intake of carbohydrates, proteins and fats.

The major sources of carbohydrates, proteins and fats are sugars, starches, alcohol, fats and oils, whole milk, cheeses, avocados, potatoes, corn, winter squash, lima beans, all frozen, canned or processed foods with sugar, sauces or fats and oils added, junk foods, chips, dips, candy, processed desserts such as pies, cakes, bakery products and ice cream, pastas such as noodles, macaroni and spaghetti.

This CALIFORNIA WEIGHT LOSS PROGRAM has been designed to automatically cut out these high calorie foods without having to spend time counting calories or using any of the other restrictive measures of fad diets, shots or pills.

The following guideline gives you a list to which to refer to assure that you are not eating more high calorie foods than you should. It is important that you continue to eat the DO EAT food from each major food group.

1. *Meats, Fish, Eggs, Beans & Nuts:*

   DO EAT: Lean meat, red meat, beef, lamb, pork, ham, veal, fish, poultry, eggs, dry beans & nuts.

   AVOID: Meat with fat showing on it, meat drippings, gravies, fried foods, foods with butter or sauces, skin on poultry, bacon, sausage, spareribs, luncheon meats, frankfurters, oils on canned fish, any type of fat added in cooking.

2. *Dairy Products:*

   DO EAT: Non-fat or low-fat milk, low-fat cheese, low-fat yogurt, diet margarines, diet desserts, diet salad dressing, buttermilk.

   AVOID: Whole milk, oils, mayonnaise,

butter, cream, sour cream, peanut butter, concentrated milk, flavoured yogurt, ice cream, all soft cheeses.

---

3. *Fruits & Vegetables:*

DO EAT: Fresh fruits and vegetables, leafy green vegetables, canned and frozen fruits and vegetables without sugar added.

AVOID: Any fruits or vegetables prepared or cooked with sugar, butter, syrup, cream sauce, cheese, salt pork or meat drippings. Avocados, starchy vegetables such as corn, lima beans, green peas, black eye peas, cowpeas or garbanzos, frozen mixed vegetables, winter squash or yellow squash, hominy grits, white potato, sweet potato, rice with butter and salt.

---

4. *Breads & Cereals:*

DO EAT: Breads, cooked or dry cereals, granola (non-sugar).

AVOID: Sweet rolls, doughnuts, bread with sugar topping, sugar-coated cereals, pies, pastries, desserts, pancakes, waffles, macaroni, noodles, spaghetti.

YOU SHOULD ALSO *AVOID* SUGARS AND ALCOHOL.

You can earn these foods by getting Weight Loss Credits. You do not need sugars or alcohol for proper nutrition. Every time you eat or drink sugar or alcohol you set back your weight loss program.

AVOID: Sugar, honey, molasses, candy, soft drinks, alcohol, syrup, cakes, cookies, pies, pastries, cupcakes, ice cream, popsicles, all packaged products with sugar added.

In other words, to assure that you are getting daily nutrition, you should balance your daily meals with portions of food from each of the four Major Food Groups and select these foods from the DO EAT list. You should avoid all other foods.

The following is a Daily Nutritional Check Off List. By eating the foods from each food group each day, you will lose weight while you learn nutritional food control at the same time. Each day you should have:

1. Meats, fish, eggs, beans & nuts:
   3 portions per day
2. Dairy products:
   2 portions per day
3. Fruits & vegetables:
   4 portions per day
4. Breads & cereals:
   2 portions per day

What Is A 'Portion' of Food?

The next problem many people have is determining the portion or amount of food they eat. Many fad diets have gone the rounds because the fad diet eliminates in many cases the problem of measuring portions. But the fad diet seriously affects the balanced food program you need to maintain vigorous health.

The problem of portions or, 'How much of a particular food should I eat?' is not really a problem at all. The answer to the question, 'How much should I have?' is really a matter of common sense. A good general rule is to cut down on your portions of meats, starches, breads, dairy products and fruits. Increase your portions of fish, green leafy vegetables and free foods such as tea, coffee, bouillon, water, raw cucumbers, celery, mushrooms and radishes. (Check the SNACK FOOD LIST on your CALIFORNIA WEIGHT LOSS PROGRAM POCKET OUTLINE.)

You must learn to control the amount of food you are eating. In the beginning, cut your portion in half of any high calorie food you are eating. Watch your weight and continue to cut your portions until you are losing weight at the rate you desire. As you continue to follow this program, you will find that you regain use of your appestat, or the mechanism that controls eating in the normal person. As you learn to eat balanced meals and you learn to eat slowly, your appestat will begin to govern the amount of food you eat. You will know when you are hungry and you will know when you are full.

One good way to cut your portions automatically, is to practice leaving some food on your plate at each meal.

When you are in doubt about how much of a particular food to eat, use the following measurements as a guideline:

liquids

    portion = One 8-ounce glass (milk), one 4-ounce glass (juices).

fruits, vegetables

    portion = One medium fruit or vegetable. With smaller fruits or vegetables, ½ cup.

meats, fish, etc.

    portion = 1/4 to 1/3 pound uncooked or 3 to 4 ounces cooked.

breads, cereals

    portion = One slice; one cup dry, ½ cup cooked.

Now there will be times when you are unsure about how much of a particular food to eat. Use your common sense and when in doubt, eat less of it than you think you should.

The following three rules are excellent for you to use to assure that you are avoiding the high calorie foods you are now eating which put on the extra weight. These rules are:

1. Cut out all processed food with sugar or butter added.
2. Avoid eating all junk food: chips, dips, etc.
3. Stick to eating fresh meats, fish, fruits and vegetables whenever possible.

THE CALIFORNIA WEIGHT LOSS PROGRAM

We recommend that you take off fat through controlling your food. You can do this by following the program which insures that you receive the proper nourishment while at the same time you lose weight. We have done all the work for you. We know how discouraging it gets when you have had to follow complex, calorie-counting programs. So we designed a weight loss program that works automatically for you.

All you have to do is follow the 15 techniques listed for you on your pocket-size WEIGHT LOSS POCKET OUTLINE. This program automatically leads you into a nutritional food control plan which guarantees you will lose weight permanently as long as you follow the program. To make it easier for you, we have eliminated the need for you to count calories, fill in daily special menus, eat only special kinds of foods or follow any other time consuming, complicated procedures.

All you have to do is follow the fifteen program steps which have been listed. The 5-Do's, the 5-Don'ts, and the 5-Do withouts. A total of only fifteen simple techniques to follow in order to lose weight permanently. We call this program the CALIFORNIA WEIGHT LOSS PROGRAM.

The 5-Do's

1. Start your weight loss program on a Monday morning. Be sure you have resolved your major stress problems. Don't start your program before a vacation, new job, move, or any other special event.

2. Complete your PERSONALITY PROFILE, WEIGHT LOSS CONTRACT, GOAL CARDS and keep a daily record of your weight on your WEIGHT LOSS CHART.

3. Eat slowly. Put your fork down between each bite. Give your mouth time to savor the flavor of your food. Enjoy yourself. Enjoy your food.

4. Chew well. Research has proved that chewing is necessary for food satisfaction. Chew each bite.

5. Increase your activity level. Burn up more energy. Get out of bed, out of your chair, out of your car. Walk more. Move around more. Get active.

The 5-Don'ts

1. Don't add salt before tasting your food. Use salt sparingly. Substitute other seasonings and spices to make food tasty.

2. Don't skip any meals.

3. Don't eat in the kitchen or anywhere else except at the table. Don't snack or eat alone if you can help it.

4. Don't eat standing up.

5. Don't keep your favorite snacking foods around the house unless they are on your WEIGHT LOSS PROGRAM SNACK FOOD LIST.

The 5-Do Withouts

1. Do without fats —
    oil, butter, margarine, mayonnaise, salad dressing, peanut butter, bacon, avocado, fried foods, oil on canned fish, visible fat on meat, any kind of fat in cooking.

2. Do without sugars —
    sugar, honey, molasses, candy, soft drinks,

sugar coated cereals, granola with sugar, all processed foods with sugar added.

3. Do without alcohol —
wine, beer, gin, vodka, bourbon, rye, whiskey, scotch, all beverages containing alcohol.

4. Do without bakery products (except bread) —
doughnuts, pies, pastries, cakes, packaged junk foods, pastas, noodles, cookies.

5. Cut in half your portions of —
beef, lamb, pork, ham, duck, goose. Remove all skin from poultry before eating. Carefully drain oil from canned fish before eating.

That's all there is to it. We have made this food control program as easy to follow as possible. By following these fifteen weight loss techniques, you will have all the ammunition you need to win your battle against being overweight.

The reasons why this program will work for you while other fad diets, shots, pills, etc., often fail, is that *while you are losing weight*, you are learning how to control your food intake nutritionally.

There are four principal 'regulators' which control your personal weight level:
- Your age
- Your size
- Your activity level
- The quantity of food you eat

The principle of controlling your food quantity is most important. Overeating = overweight. But it isn't quite that simple because there are some foods you can eat all day and not put on weight and others that contain 'dynamite' in high calorie content.

We have listed most of these 'dynamite' foods on what we call a SET-BACK FOOD LIST. This makes it simple for you. Just check the SET-BACK FOOD LIST and if you find a food on it you want to eat, you know that by eating it you are going to set back your weight loss program.

With all foods not on the SET-BACK FOOD LIST, simply use common sense in deciding how much of that food to eat at any one meal. Use the guidelines already suggested in this lesson and use the Rule of One.

The Rule of One

This rule says you have just one portion of each food you eat at each meal. In most cases this is easy. For example at each meal just have one slice of cheese or one egg or one lamb chop or one spoonful of rice or one apple, orange, or pear.

For those foods like stews, casseroles, spaghetti or anything not easily measured in units of 'one' eat one half of the amount you are eating now.

Daily Rewards

Record your weight at the same time each day. On each day that you lose one or more pounds or do not gain one or more pounds, pay yourself with a Weight Loss Credit. As soon as you have earned two Weight Loss Credits, pay yourself (if you want to) with one portion of one of the foods you enjoy which is listed on the SET-BACK FOODS LIST.

Remember: every time you eat a set-back food, it will set back your weight loss program. The more set-back foods you eat, the longer it will take you to lose weight. For example, suppose you lose two pounds today and don't gain anything tomorrow. You can credit yourself with two Weight Loss Credits and you can have one portion of ice cream, cake, avocado, baked potato, a drink of rum, vodka, gin, or any food listed on the SET-BACK FOOD LIST.

The important thing to remember is that you cannot earn more than one Weight Loss Credit per day and you cannot eat more than one portion (as listed) of only one set-back food you select from the list. There is no way you can earn two or more set-back foods as a reward for having earned two Weight Loss Credits.

This means you cannot 'save up' your Weight Loss Credits and go on a food binge. Each time you have eaten one set-back food, you must eliminate all of the Weight Loss Credits you have earned and start over again.

Food control is your key to success. People with weight problems are like bad drivers who have not learned how to control the car they drive. Sooner or later, the bad driver runs into trouble, either a ticket for speeding or a bad accident. Control is your key to effective weight loss. Learn to control food and you learn to use food as a tool rather than have food use you.

Starting Your Program

During the first week, follow the fifteen rules exactly. During the second week, add one set-back food per day to your daily program, if you feel you need it. Use your Weight Loss Credits to pay yourself with other set-back foods if you like. Use the Rule of One to cut back the amount of each food you are eating. When in doubt, eat only one half of what you are eating. If you still find you are not losing weight, cut your amount by another one third.

You now have everything you need to successfully lose weight. In the next lesson we are going to cover other helpful techniques you can use to speed up your program and become the slim, healthy person you want to be.

DO NOT GO ON TO LESSON NINE
UNTIL TOMORROW

Controlled fasting and other helpful techniques

Control the quantity and quality of what you eat

When you have finally mastered your control over food, you will be able to eat whatever you want. You will not have to fear desserts or baked potatoes oozing with butter and sour cream. You will enjoy the delight of being able to taste many pleasures which come from food without the excess weight which comes from being unable to control the quantity and quality of the food you eat.

Controlled Fasting

Fasting is an ancient tradition; properly used, it can be effective in mastering food control. No one should practice fasting without first checking it out with their doctor. Once you reach your weight loss level, fasting is an excellent way to maintain that weight loss objective.

We have developed what we call *controlled fast ing*. This is a way to counteract those times when you overeat or celebrate with 'too much Thanksgiving dinner', etc.. Controlled fasting consists of substituting for one meal liquids including tea, coffee and water and one portion of either meat, fish or eggs. You may also snack on any of the foods listed on your SNACK FOOD LIST.

You should not substitute controlled fasting for more than one meal at a time. We recommend you start your weight loss program by using controlled fasting no more than three times a week. Select the meal you enjoy most and then substitute controlled fasting for one of the other meals of the day. For example, if you are a big breakfast eater, go ahead and have your normal breakfast but substitute controlled fasting for your lunch or dinner. Don't use controlled fasting as a punishment. Use it as a power resource you can apply to lose weight. You will find it a pleasant way to control the food you eat. The important thing is not to overdo it. Never use controlled fasting for more than one meal at a time.

Remember, your objective is *permanent* weight loss and *permanent* food control, not the yo-yo temporary weight loss that comes from unusual or fad diets.

Other Helpful Techniques
1. *Vegetables*
The following two rules will help you master control of vegetables:

A. You can eat all the vegetables you like and as much of these vegetables as you like except for those vegetables that fall into the following categories:

(a) HIGHEST IN CALORIES — potatoes, corn, lima beans — eat only one of these per week.

(b) HIGH IN CALORIES — carrots, peas, beets, winter squash — eat only two of these per week.

B. Double your portion of salads and greens during your weight loss program. Use low calorie salad dressing and only one spoonful.

2. *Water*

Water is your best friend. You can use water to tremendous advantage to lose weight. Fill yourself up with a glass of ice water before a meal. Take a drink of water before you feel yourself getting hungry. Use water to cut down your appetite.

3. *Your DAILY REINFORCEMENT CARDS*

In the back of this program there is a set of printed weight loss techniques, which we call DAILY REINFORCEMENT CARDS. You can cut them out in order to use them more easily. They also add some fun to the program.

There is no way in a short period of time you can remember everything contained in this weight loss program. Each of these cards contains an excellent technique you can use to reach your weight loss goal. Select a different one each morning. Use the technique suggested to make your program work that day. On the next day, select another. When you have gone through all of them, mix them up and start all over again. This gives you an easy, effective method to reinforce your knowledge of these techniques and concentrate on one of them each day. It provides variety and gives you an additional back-up system to use to succeed.

4. *Other Helpful Techniques*

a. EAT SLOWLY

- put a cardboard sign on the table in front of you to remind you to eat slowly
- put your fork down between each bite
- don't put food in your mouth when there is still some food in your mouth
- cut your food into smaller bites

b. CHEW WELL

- chewing food gives you satisfaction
- you enjoy your meals more when you chew your food
- include food you must chew with each meal

c. ENJOY YOUR WEIGHT LOSS PROGRAM

- use attractive table settings
- garnish your plate with colorful food arrangements
- use smaller plates, add parsley, cherry tomatoes, lemon or orange wedges
- use a wine glass for smaller amounts of liquid

d. NIBBLE LOW CALORIE FOODS

- try raw vegetables such as mushrooms, celery, sliced cucumber, zucchini, cherry tomatoes, cauliflower

e. LEARN TO STOP EATING BEFORE YOU ARE FULL

- eat larger meals in the morning
- eat smaller meals in the evening before you go to sleep

f. MAKE YOUR FOOD TASTY

- use herbs, spices and seasonings to make plain foods fit for a gourmet
- use wine to flavour your food when cooking it
- use fresh fruits, vegetables, meats and fish whenever possible instead of canned or frozen food

g. WHEN EATING OUT

- be careful of portion sizes. Ask for a children's plate or for half portions of food
- watch out for sauces, gravies and dressings — they are apt to conceal much added fat
- order wine vinegar or lemon juice for your green or tossed salads
- trim all visible fat from meat. Skin the chicken or turkey before eating it
- order an iced tea or a non-alcoholic drink unless you have earned enough Weight Loss Credits for liquor or wine

h. WHEN YOU BLOW IT AND GO ON A FOOD BINGE

- binge for only one meal
- don't feel guilty about it

- pick up and go on
- start back on your program the next meal

i. DO NOT SKIP ANY MEALS

- it's easier to control your eating if you are not excessively hungry

j. REMOVE ALL 'JUNK FOOD' FROM AROUND THE HOUSE

- don't tempt yourself
- get rid of foods like chips, dips, candy, desserts, crackers, salted nuts and bakery goods

k. SHOP CAREFULLY

- plan your meals around the fresh meats, fish, fruits, and vegetables which are available

l. DON'T BE DISCOURAGED BY A WEIGHT LOSS PLATEAU

- Sooner or later you will hit a period when you don't seem to be losing weight. Usually, this is related to an adjustment in the water level balance in your body. Don't get discouraged. Hang in there. Usually, after a while you will lose three, four, or five pounds all at once and then go on losing at your normal speed.

m. READ THE LABELS ON ALL THE FOODS YOU BUY

- avoid all packaged foods that contain sugar

Summary

You now have a complete weight loss program to follow. It is a sound and nutritional program and you can lose weight permanently on it by following it. The time it takes you to lose your weight is up to you. Even if you fail this time or are not ready yet to lose weight or want to put off your weight loss program until after you resolve a major stress situation in your life, you have still completed the groundwork it takes to launch your own successful program.

You now have a set of objective systems you can use to reach your weight loss goal. You don't have to 'go it alone'. These techniques will work for you whenever you put them to work.

We have included a list of questions and answers to many problems people have when losing weight. If you find you are having a problem with your program, check the list to see if a solution is there for you. If you find yourself losing steam in the middle of your program, go back and start this program all over again. Begin with Lesson One and read a lesson a day until you get back in the swing of it.

Good luck and good living. We guarantee you will enjoy yourself, your life, your friends and your food much, much more after you have slimmed down to the weight you should be and have mastered your control of food.

You *can* do it. The *time* it takes you to get it done is up to you.

Questions and Answers

How can I control my sudden cravings for fattening foods?

In the beginning, you may not be able to control these sudden 'compulsions' to stuff yourself with fattening foods. Remember, by losing weight, you are changing your personality. Your fat self is going to fight back. The sudden cravings may be more powerful than your will to resist. The secret is not to get discouraged when you give in to your craving for food. Try to limit the fattening foods you eat during an attack. If you stick with your program, read your goals, and persist, you will find that the cravings come less and less often.

How does my fat self fight back?

Your fat self will fight back any way it can. You may get headaches, shooting pains, nausea, dizziness, fear that your weight loss is going to cause you to get sick, constipation, and loss of energy. Don't fear these symptoms. If you are at all worried, see your doctor. Remember, losing weight is one of the best preventions against illness you can take. Ignore your fat self and usually these symptoms will go away.

Why do I seem to fail on diets? It is as if I am working against myself.

You *are* working against yourself. For a long period of time your eating habits and your psychological habits have made you gain weight. A habit is part of your personality; it gives a reward. Therefore, in changing this habit, you are making a psychological as well as a physical change. The self you are working against is the fat self. The key to your success in changing is to persist in spite of temporary failures. Don't let yourself be pulled back into your old habit patterns.

Is it possible I am just one of those people who cannot lose weight no matter what weight loss program I am on?

It is *possible*, but not probable. If you suspect you have a glandular or thyroid or physical problem which may keep you from losing weight, see your doctor. You will know immediately whether or not this is true.

How do I take fat off unwanted places? How do I slim my stomach and other bulges?

After you have reached your desired weight level, a combination of continued 'controlled' eating and mild exercise can reduce the bulges. But remember, be sure your actual objective is weight loss and not the fountain of youth. Don't try to be 20 if you are 40. Accept yourself as you are.

How can I control the terrible hunger and appetite pangs I get when I am trying to lose weight?

Remember, water is your best friend. Drink a full glass of water whenever you get a chance. Be sure not to skip any meals. Eat before you get hungry. Snack from the approved SNACK FOOD LIST. But most important, your psychological attitude toward your weight loss program will stop those hunger pangs. If you are consistently reaching your goals, and you really want to lose weight, you won't have the psychological craving or need for food that you may have had in the past.

What are some of the ways I can succeed on this program when I am weak or depressed or about to fail?

Substitution is your key to success. If you have filled out your PERSONALITY PROFILE, you should know when your weak moments will come along. At those times substitute other activities for your usual routine. Take a walk instead of sitting down in front of the T.V.. Get out of the house instead of reading a book. Make a list of things you've always wanted to do but haven't done and do them instead of eating. Start a new hobby. Take a night course. Instead of wolfing down a piece of pie, start painting a picture or practicing your new guitar or go out and hit golf balls. If you feel you are about to go off on a food binge, postpone the eating binge for a specific time (one hour). This gives you a second chance to decide whether you really want to give in. Often you will find something else to do and forget about your hunger cravings.

What can I do when I get really discouraged?

You must fight your discouragement, but let's face it, there will be some days when you are so discouraged you will rush to the refrigerator and stuff yourself with food. Well, don't quit just because you've failed. Don't let a 10-minute failure destroy days or weeks of success. We all have our bad days. We all fail from time to time. You are not perfect and neither am I. The Olympic track star got there only through failure. Learn to live a day at a time. Learn to overlook yesterday's failures. Consistency makes this program work. Remember, this program includes temporary failure. We know you are not perfect. (Remember the illustration of real failure as opposed to failure on the way to success). Keep plugging along day by day and you will reach your goal. When you get discouraged, remember that it will pass. Live through it, fight through it, be patient.

How can I be sure that this time this weight loss program will work for me?

You can't be sure. It may be that you really don't want to lose weight. It may be that you have other problems and your weight is just a symptom. The point is that you now have a tested program to follow if you really want to lose weight this time. If you still find yourself failing, perhaps you do need some outside help. A lot of people give up just when they are about to succeed. If you feel like quitting, tell yourself you will quit after you have given yourself 'just one more day'. Keep going day by day until you no longer want to quit.

Can I lose weight and keep on drinking?

Probably not, at least if you are a 'social drinker' who has more than one or two drinks a day. Any time you have alcoholic drinks you change yourself. Usually the change is just enough to dull your new motivation to lose weight. Your old habits become more powerful than the new ones you are establishing. You give in to one cracker and cheese, one slice of bread with dinner and finally just 'one piece of pie'. If you want to lose weight fast, stop drinking during your weight loss program. If you find you are not able to stop drinking, it may be that you have a drinking problem, not a weight problem. If on the other hand, you simply don't want to give up the pleasure of a drink or two, try your weight loss program and include the drinks and see if you lose weight. Your WEIGHT LOSS CHART will tell you whether you can keep on drinking and lose weight. Excessive drinking can lead to depression and depression can lead to excessive eating.

What exercise is best for me?

We have intentionally left out exercises in this weight loss program. Proper exercising is vital to maintaining excellent health. However, it is also vital that you get a clear 'go ahead' from your doctor as to the exercise program you select. You do not have to exercise to lose weight but it does help greatly and increases the rate at which you lose pounds. You should exercise daily to maintain good health. We advise that you work up an exercise program with your doctor. Walking is one of the best exercises there is and it can be done anywhere. Swimming is an excellent exercise. Depending upon your age and your physical condition, you should work up a sensible, enjoyable exercise program for yourself.

Should I share my weight loss program objectives with anyone else?

Generally, you should not share your specific

objectives with anyone. This program is designed to assist you in losing weight in the privacy of your own home. You should share with your family and doctor your intention to lose weight on this program and the rewards you have selected to pay yourself with as you meet your objectives. Do not share your PERSONALITY PROFILE information with anyone. This is your program. Work on it by yourself.

What should I do if my family or friends laugh at me?

If either your family or your friends try to discourage you from losing excess weight, you have a real problem to solve. It means they want you to stay just the way you are. This means you have to make a choice between what you want and what they want. Since it is your life, we recommend you choose to do what you want. If you have taken control of your own mind, you should not let their laughter bother you. In many cases, once you really show them that this time you are serious, they will stop laughing after they see the results of your efforts.

If I really start to slide back into my old habits after succeeding at first, what should I do?

Read your weight loss program through from the beginning again. Start with Lesson One and reread a lesson a day just like you did when you first started this program. Eat your meals at a different time. Get away for a weekend if you can. Find something exciting to do that you haven't ever done before. Read your GOAL CARDS more often. Start a new hobby. Make your life more interesting.

PERSONALITY PROFILE

SECTION #1

NAME _____ AGE _____

OCCUPATION _____ EDUCATION _____

MARRIED__ SINGLE__ DIVORCED__ NO. OF CHILDREN__

HEIGHT____WEIGHT____WEIGHT LOSS GOAL_____

HOBBIES/INTERESTS _____

ANY MAJOR ILLNESS DURING LAST YEAR _____

HOSPITALIZED_____ DOCTOR _____

BEST FRIEND OUTSIDE FAMILY_____

1. How long have you been fat? _____

2. When did you first get fat? _____

3. Was your family fat? _____

4. What caused you to get fat? _____

_____

5. Have you ever tried to lose weight before? _____

6. Why did you fail?_____

SECTION #2

1. Why do you keep on overeating? _____

2. How fat are you? _____

3. What foods do you eat most? _____

_____

4. What foods do you like most? _____

_____

5. What rewards do you think you are getting from over-eating?
   - ☐ I substitute food for loneliness
   - ☐ I face emotional problems by eating food
   - ☐ I escape a dull life through food
   - ☐ I kill time by eating food
   - ☐ I fight fear by eating food
   - ☐ My family and friends expect me to be fat
   - ☐ I look younger when I am fat
   - ☐ I love to eat rich, high calorie foods
   - ☐ Food calms my nerves
   - ☐ I don't like myself and food comforts me
   - ☐ I don't have any real friends so I eat food
   - ☐ Nobody cares if I am fat so why not be fat
   - ☐ My family has always been fat and so am I
   - ☐ I have no will power, I am weak

6. What other rewards do you think you are getting?

   _____

7. Are you a heavy drinker?_____

8. Are you addicted to any other drugs?_____

9. Are there any major personal problems you are finding it difficult to cope with?

   _____

10. Is being fat your *real* problem? _____

11. Do you love yourself? _____

12. Are you afraid of anything or anyone?_____

13. Do you feel 'trapped' by life? _____

14. Is your marriage satisfying? _____

15. Is your life exciting? _____

16. Can you think of any major frustrations you may have? _____

17. Are you insecure? _____

18. Is your weight a compensation for sexual frustration?
_____

19. Are you a fast eater? _____

20. Are you happy with your present career?_____

21. Do you ever go on food binges (stuffing yourself with food even when not hungry)?
_____

22. Do you snack between meals?_____

23. Who are your best friends? _____
_____

24. Is there anyone who doesn't like you? _____
_____

    Why?_____

25. What are your friends like (are they fat too)?_____

26. Do you admit you have a weight problem? _____

27. Do you get cravings for certain foods? _____

    If so, what foods? _____
_____

    When do you get these cravings? _____

28. How do you normally feel?
    □ Excited by life   □ Secure
    □ Dull   □ Hemmed in
    □ Anxious   □ Relaxed
    □ Overworked   □ Young
    □ Joyful   □ Happy
    □ Positive   □ Content
    □ Optimistic   □ Old

□ Confident	□ Feeling of failure
□ Afraid	□ Feeling of success
□ Tired	□ Going nowhere
□ Alert, curious	□ In love with life
□ Bored by life	□ Hopeful
□ Vigorous, healthy	□ At peace with the world
□ Sick	□ Insecure

29. Do you control your own mind (if not, who does)?

_____

30. Do you have any fear of the following kind:
    - □ Fear of poverty
    - □ Fear of losing a friend, loved one, child
    - □ Fear of failure
    - □ Fear of death
    - □ Fear of growing old
    - □ Fear of losing youth
    - □ Fear of sickness
    - □ Fear of pain
    - □ Fear of strangers

31. Do you crave food after an unpleasant emotional experience?

_____

SECTION #3

1. Why do you want to lose weight? _____

_____

2. What rewards do you get from losing weight?
    - □ I feel healthier
    - □ I look more attractive
    - □ I am more respected
    - □ I have less chance for illness
    - □ I have a much better mental attitude toward life
    - □ I am at my natural weight
    - □ I look better to my family and friends
    - □ I have a better chance of living longer
    - □ I look younger
    - □ I sleep better

95

- I have more opportunities open in life
- I save money I can use on other things
- I have more energy
- I substitute more interesting activities for eating food
- I improve my earning capacity
- I have a much better opinion of myself
- I make my life more interesting and exciting
- I improve my self control

3. What other rewards will you get?

_____

_____

4. Do you really want to lose weight?_____

5. Are you willing to earn change by paying a price?

_____

6. Does your family want you to change? _____

_____

7. Can you think of anyone who doesn't want you to change?

_____

8. Are you willing to change?

SECTION #4

1. Are you now absolutely sure you want to change?_____

2. What rewards do you want from losing weight?

_____

_____

_____

_____

_____

_____

_____

3. Are they more attractive to you than the rewards you are now getting from being fat?

_____

4. Are you willing to persist in spite of temporary failure from time to time?

_____

5. Are you ready to create your own personal plan for losing weight?

_____

REINFORCEMENT CARDS

Each card contains a specific weight loss technique designed to help you lose weight. Use the cards any way you like. Review them daily or shuffle the cards and select a single card each day. Concentrate on practicing the technique on each card until you *automatically* use all these techniques to control food *permanently*.

cut out

USE FRUIT

When you have an urge to snack on fattening foods, candy, ice cream, sweets, SUBSTITUTE AN APPLE, BANANA, ORANGE, PEAR OR PEACH. You get real nutrition plus natural sugar. It lifts you without the "empty fattening calories" of the other snacks.

AVOID THE SET-BACK FOODS

Think of your weight loss program as a trip. You decide how slowly or quickly you will get to the end of the trip by the way you use your "energy." Avoid the set-back foods and you will get there five times as fast as you would if you don't.

PAMPER YOURSELF

Treat yourself like a VIP. Stop running yourself down. Enjoy your life. Take more time to pamper yourself. No matter what your situation, you personally can improve it by pushing yourself less and enjoying life more.

TAKE A WALK

Substitute walking for eating. Walking is one of the best possible exercises. Remember, your activity level is one of the four major controllers of your weight. Try walking out your frustrations instead of eating them away.

LOVE YOURSELF

Most of us give everyone else a break but not ourselves. You are a wonderful creation with as much right as anyone else to enjoy your experience here on earth. Put yourself first and love yourself. Don't try to be perfect and forget past failures.

GET ACTIVE

Stop lying around in bed. Stop sitting around. Stop driving every place you go. *Get active*. Start slowly and build up your activity level. Spend energy. Don't do it in fits and starts, do it daily.

BE A CHILD

Don't be an adult all the time. Do some of the childlike things you used to do. Do some foolish things. Be daring. Skip down the street. Sing in the shower. Tease someone. Be a child for a little while.

JUST THIS TIME

When you've tried everything and just can't resist the refrigerator raid, tell yourself you'll do it just this time. Think yourself through this one challenge. Even if you only postpone your food binge for a few minutes, you've shown yourself that *you can consciously control your food intake*.

PUNCH A PILLOW

Try punching out your frustrations with a pillow or better yet a punching bag. It's good exercise and it doesn't put on weight.

- - - - - - - - - - - - - - - - - - -

CHANGE YOUR PATTERNS

Find out when you are most tempted to eat fattening foods and do something else at that time. Change your dinner hour. Get out of the house. Take a walk. Go for a swim. Change your pattern of living to eliminate the temptation to overeat.

- - - - - - - - - - - - - - - - - - -

EAT SLOWLY

Chew your food completely. Savour each bite. Put your fork down between each bite. *Slow down.* Don't eat standing up. Be aware of what you are eating and how you are eating it.

EAT ALONE

Practice eating a meal alone. Spend the meal thinking about how you eat and why you eat what you do. Watch yourself eating. Really think about what you are doing.

ASK YOURSELF "WHAT DO I NEED?"

When you find yourself hit by a hunger craving, ask yourself what it is you really need. Are you really hungry — or are you stuffing yourself because of an emotional stress? Try to face your real problem and resolve it without using food.

ASK YOURSELF "WHO IS IN CONTROL?"

Habits are automatic actions. Stop and think about what you are doing. Take mental control of yourself. Tell yourself you are in conscious control of your actions. Break the automatic habit response.

ASK YOURSELF
"WHY AM I DOING THIS?"

Before you "give in" to a food binge or in any other way go off your food control program, ask yourself, "Why?" Try to think about why you want to set back your weight loss program. Try to come up with the real reason you are turning to food.

FOCUS ON THE PRESENT

Are you "eating without thinking about it?" Are you rushing around? Stop and bring yourself right into the present. *Be aware of this moment.* Clear your mind of all past regrets and future worries. Stop and use your mental control, not your past habits, to determine what you are doing.

REWARD YOURSELF DAILY

Don't wait until you are slim to be slim. Reward yourself each day with something other than food that you enjoy. Be kind to yourself. Don't push yourself so hard. Be tolerant of your weaknesses. REWARD YOURSELF.

COUNT TO 10

Break a food binge by at least counting to ten slowly before you stuff yourself. The key point is that if you can resist the urge to eat immediately when it hits you, you will ultimately resist it permanently.

ANTICIPATE

Plan ahead! Take a glass of water *before you get hungry*. Eat before you get hungry. Don't starve yourself into a food binge. Stop looking at food as the enemy. It's not food that makes you fat, it's the way you eat it.

USE WATER

Use liquids to control hunger cravings. Drink water, tea, coffee, bouillon before a meal, before you get hungry. Try a glass of ice tea instead of a cocktail before dinner. Water can be your best friend.

TAPE PHOTOS TO REFRIGERATOR

Cut out magazine photos showing you the way you want to look. Cut out photos of your daily and special rewards. Tape the photos to the refrigerator and in other places around the house. Change the photos often. They help you reinforce your new weight loss rewards and goals.

VISUALIZE IN DETAIL

See yourself slim. See yourself being rewarded. Don't just quickly "think about" your new weight level. Close your eyes and see it, taste it, smell it, daydream it. Keep a vivid mental image of the new rewards you are getting from being slim.

CUT OUT FATS AND SALT

Don't salt your food before you eat it. Cut all fats from your food the first week and pay yourself with Weight Loss Credits from then on. Use other spices and seasonings to give your food "gourmet" taste.

SUBSTITUTE

Think up other ways to face emotional stress. Substitute walking, drinking water, going to a movie, visiting a friend. Pay yourself with things you enjoy doing. Be kind to yourself. Substitute things you enjoy doing for eating.

RELAX QUIETLY

Once a day, get away to a quiet dark room and relax. Lie down. Take a deep breath, count to ten, exhale and imagine all your tensions leaving your body. Repeat the process and count to eight, to seven, and down to the point where you are breathing regularly.

STOCK SNACK FOODS

Keep plenty of non-fattening foods in your refrigerator. Carrot sticks, celery, cucumbers, onions, tomatoes. Munch on these instead of prepared or packaged "junk food."

SHATTER YOUR REWARD

When you are tempted to eat a SET-BACK FOOD, stop, close your eyes and see your new weight loss goals and rewards being "shattered." Do this every time you are tempted to eat a fattening food.

THINK SLIM

Don't wait until you are slim to think slim. Start planning the new clothes you are going to buy. Start moving about more. Think like a slim person. Think of yourself as a slim person. Eliminate all negative thoughts about yourself. Think slim and get the rewards of being slim before you actually get there.

REHEARSE YOUR WAY TO SUCCESS

While relaxing, rehearse yourself resisting the temptation to eat fattening foods. Rehearse yourself saying "no" and sticking to your food control program. If you fail, rehearse the same situation but succeed in your mental rehearsal.

GOAL CARD

Name: _____

Goal: _____

_____

_____

_____

_____

_____

GOAL CARD

Name: _____

Goal: _____

_____

_____

_____

_____

_____

GOAL CARD

Name: _____

Goal: _____

_____

_____

_____

_____

GOAL CARD

Name: _____

Goal: _____

_____

_____

_____

_____

- - - - - - - - - - - - - - - - - - - -

GOAL CARD

Name: _____

Goal: _____

_____

_____

_____

_____

- - - - - - - - - - - - - - - - - - - -

GOAL CARD

Name: _____

Goal: _____

_____

_____

_____

THE 5-POINT CALIFORNIA WEIGHT LOSS PROGRAM

Carry this easy-reference POCKET OUTLINE with you wherever you go. Refer to it often until you have memorized the three rules and fifteen steps to *permanent weight loss.*

THE THREE RULES

1. Control the *amount* of food you eat.
2. Eat slowly; sit down and chew every bite you eat.
3. Cut way down on the fats, sugar and salt you eat.

THE 5 DO'S

1. Start your weight loss program on Monday morning. Make sure you have resolved your major stress problems.
2. Complete your PERSONALITY PROFILE, WEIGHT LOSS CONTRACT and GOAL CARDS.
3. Eat slowly. Chew well. Put your fork down between each bite. Enjoy your food. Don't wolf it down.
4. Reward yourself daily! Reward yourself with foods you love when you have earned two or more Weight Loss Credits.
5. Increase your activity level. Burn up more energy. Move around.

THE 5 DON'TS

1. Don't add salt before tasting your food.
2. Don't skip any meals.
3. Don't eat in the kitchen or eat standing up. Don't snack alone if you can help it.
4. Don't keep your favorite snacking foods around the house if they are on the SET-BACK FOOD LIST.
5. Don't get discouraged after giving in to a food binge. Start right back into your weight loss program and don't feel guilty about slipping.

THE 5 DO WITHOUTS

1. Do without fats.
2. Do without sugars.
3. Do without alcohol.
4. Do without bakery products (except bread).
5. Cut in half your portions of: beef, lamb, pork, ham, duck, goose. Remove all skin from poultry before eating. Drain oil from canned fish.

SNACK FOOD LIST

Drink tea, iced or hot, bouillon, clear broth, coffee, water. Eat cucumber slices, celery sticks, radishes, raw zucchini with low calorie dressing, sour or dill pickles, green onions, mushrooms, salad greens, parsley, alfalfa sprouts, bean sprouts, cabbage, D-Zerta, rhubarb, watercress.

SET-BACK FOODS LIST

Every time you eat one of these foods you set back your weight loss program. Earn these foods by earning two or more Weight Loss Credits. Eat these set-back foods only in the amounts listed here after each food.

Almonds (5 medium chocolate covered)
Almonds (12 salted)
Avocado (¼ medium-sized)
Biscuits (1)
Beer (1 small can)
Butter (2 pats or 2 teaspoons)
Cashews (8)
Caramels (2 small pieces)
Candy (1 small piece)
Cookies (2 small)
Crackers (5)
Champagne (1 small glass or 5 ounces)
Corn (1 ear or 1 cup)
Doughnuts (1 plain)
Fig newtons (2)
Gravy (2 tablespoons)
Hash brown potatoes (2 tablespoons)
Ice Cream (1 scoop or single cone)
Jelly/Jam (1 level tablespoon)
Kidney beans (2 tablespoons)
Lima beans (2 tablespoons)
Macaroni (2 tablespoons)
Navy beans (2 tablespoons)
Noodles (2 tablespoons)
Muffins (1)
Liquor (1 shot or 1½ ounces)
Pie (½ piece)
Peanut butter (1 level tablespoon)
Popcorn (2 cups plain, unbuttered)
Potato chips (10)
Peanuts (20)
Pretzels (8 small)
Pudding (½ cup)
Pea Soup (½ cup)
Pancakes (1 large)
Rolls (1)
Raisins (2 tablespoons)
Sweet wine (¼ cup)

White wine (1 small 5-ounce glass)
Sweet potatoes (1 very small)
Baked potatoes (½ medium)
Tomato soup (1 cup)
Waffles (½)
Tortillas (1)
French bread (1 slice, 1 butter pat)
Fruits canned in sugar (½ cup)

WEIGHT LOSS CHART

NAME _____   DATE _____

DAYS

WEIGHT	1	2	3	4	5	6	7	8	9	10	11	12	13	14	15	16	17	18	19	20	21	22	23	24	25	26	27	28	29	30	31

START

WEIGHT LOSS CHART

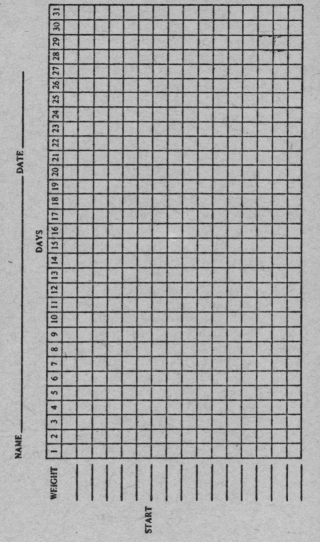

NAME. _____ DATE. _____

WEIGHT	1	2	3	4	5	6	7	8	9	10	11	12	13	14	15	16	17	18	19	20	21	22	23	24	25	26	27	28	29	30	31

DAYS

START

WEIGHT LOSS CHART

NAME _____   DATE _____

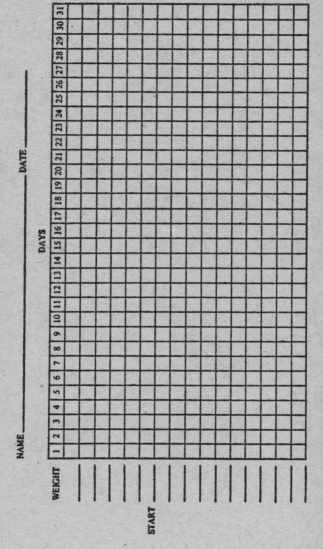